Allama Mashriqi:
A Founder of Islamia College
(Peshawar, Pakistan)

Allama Mashriqi:
A Founder of Islamia College
(Peshawar, Pakistan)

In Celebration of Islamia College's
Platinum Jubilee (1913-2013)

Nasim Yousaf

Published by:
AMZ Publications
New York, USA

I extend my cordial thanks to the authors of all the publications that I referenced in compiling this work.

Table of Contents

About Allama Mashriqi

From Nasim Yousaf's article entitled Allama Mashriqi — A Giant Among Men.

Allama Inayatullah Khan Al-Mashriqi was born on August 25, 1888. Mashriqi obtained his initial education at home and then attended school in Amritsar, prior to joining Foreman Christian College (F.C. College) in Lahore. He obtained his Masters degree in Mathematics in first class from the University of Punjab and later went on to study at the University of Cambridge. Throughout his academic life, Mashriqi made history; it is believed that his academic records at the University of Cambridge - where he completed four Triposes within five years with distinction - are yet to be broken.

Upon completion of his studies, Mashriqi joined Islamia College (Peshawar) as Vice Principal, and was later appointed Under Secretary at the Education Department of the Government of British India. In light of emerging differences with the British, he was demoted to Headmaster of Government High School in Peshawar. During his tenure in Government Service, he was offered Knighthood and Ambassadorship to Afghanistan, but declined both offers, as he considered them a means for the British authorities to use him for their own political purposes.

While in Government service, Mashriqi wrote *Tazkirah*, a scientific commentary on the Holy Koran, which was nominated for the Nobel Prize. When the Nobel Prize Committee asked him to translate the book into any major European language, he declined to do so; he considered this to be an insult to the millions of people who spoke the Urdu language. Admiring Mashriqi and *Tazkirah*, Air Marshal (Retd.) Qazi Javed Ahmed wrote (in a message to me), "I am an admirer of Allama sahib and have read some of his books…I have also read his two volumes of 'Tazkira'…He is so relevant even today and we can all draw inspiration and guidance from what he has written."

In 1930, Mashriqi founded the Khaksar Tehrik (Khaksar Movement) to revive the glory of the nation. However, the British became wary of the Movement's ultimate goal, which was predicated on ending British rule in order to bring freedom to India. Thus, the Tehrik was banned in Punjab in 1940 and Mashriqi was imprisoned. In 1941, the ban on the Movement was expanded throughout the entire India. The Government of British India demanded that Mashriqi disband his movement, or continue to remain behind bars. However, Mashriqi refused to succumb to any threat and replied that the Khaksar Movement was not his personal property that he could dispose off. The British, therefore, continued to imprison him for an extended period of time; he faced all atrocities with extraordinary courage and remained steadfast. In fact, Mashriqi fasted for 80 days in jail to protest his unjust imprisonment; he was ultimately released, but his movements remained restricted.

Following Mashriqi's release from prison, he vigorously began working for an end to British rule. He was warned many times by the British authorities to halt his activities, but he did not waver in his resolve. In 1945, he presented *The Constitution of Free India, 1946, A.C.,* which provided protection for the rights of both Muslims and non-Muslims, and could serve as a precursor to jointly seeking independence. Unfortunately, the document was not adopted for political reasons.

Mashriqi continued his efforts until British rule in India came to an end in 1947. Despite achieving independence, Mashriqi was saddened by the division of India. To him, partition was not the solution to the country's problems.

Allama Mashriqi died at Albert Victor Hospital (Mayo Hospital) in Lahore on August 27, 1963. A pall of gloom prevailed across the country following his tragic death; condolence messages from followers and admirers came from all over the world. Mashriqi's funeral prayers were led by Maulana Abdus Sattar Khan Niazi at Badshahi Mosque in Lahore. All along the funeral procession, the public gathered to pay tributes to their leader and showered his body with flowers.

Mashriqi left behind a lasting legacy of combating injustice, communalism, and sectarianism. He worked all his life for unity, discipline, and fostering a peaceful co-existence among people, regardless of religion, class, color or creed. As a result of his unrelenting fight, he forever changed the history of the Indian subcontinent; Mashriqi's vision of co-existence needs to be followed in order to bring peace to the world today.

Mashriqi's Thoughts on Education

Allama Mashriqi believed that a nation could not rise without education, and emphasized the power of education throughout his career. From the very beginning, he set an example for others to follow by breaking academic records at the University of Punjab and the University of Cambridge.

Subsequently, he eschewed more lucrative job offers to pursue a career as an educationist. Even among his own family, he ensured that his daughters (not just his sons) obtained an education, at a time when female education was not commonplace. His progressive thought process was reflected in his work at Islamia College, where he helped revolutionize the system by bringing about an educational awakening among the males and females in the North West Frontier Province. In his later years, Mashriqi continued advocating for the power of education. In 1951, he sent a message to scientists of the world ("Human Problem") to continue to expand their knowledge and in 1955 to the Government of Pakistan to establish a scientific institute in Karachi. He asked the masses for donations to the latter cause. Even in death, Mashriqi's commitment to education remained steadfast; his Will stipulated that a portion of his wealth should be used to grant scholarships to outstanding students.

Allama Mashriqi: A Founder of Islamia College (Peshawar, Pakistan)

In Celebration of Islamia College's Platinum Jubilee (1913-2013)

Introduction

Islamia College was founded in Peshawar 100 years ago. The founding fathers and pioneering team of the college were Nawab Sir Sahibzada Abdul Qayyum, Sir George Roos-Keppel,[1] L. Tipping, and Allama Mashriqi. As the very first Vice Principal (and later Principal) of Islamia College, Allama Mashriqi had a remarkable academic career in his own right. He excelled during his studies at the University of Cambridge and came to Islamia College to change the face of education in the region. During his tenure, the College emerged as a symbol of academic excellence and pride for *Pashtoons*. And over the years, it grew to become one the finest institutions

---

[1] Sir George Roos-Keppel was the Chief Commissioner (equivalent to Governor) of the North West Frontier Province (NWFP). NWFP was considered a Chief Commissioner Province in 1901; in 1932, it became a Governor Province.

in Pakistan and brought about a revolution for education in the province.

Mashriqi's Educational Background

Inayatullah Khan, famously known as Allama Mashriqi, distinguished himself academically at an early age. While studying at the University of Cambridge, Mashriqi obtained four Triposes in five years with distinction, an unprecedented feat! The British media paid high tributes to Mashriqi on his achievements at Cambridge. Newspapers such as *The Times, London* (June 17, 1911), *The Daily Mirror* (June 17, 1911), *Indian Student* (London, June 30, 1911), *The Daily Chronicle* (London, 1912), *The Cambridge Daily* (June 12, 1912), *Westminster Gazette* (June 12, 1912), and *The Yorkshire Post* (June 13, 1912)[2] published news regarding his academic accolades. *The Star* (London, 1912) wrote: "It was hitherto considered not possible at Cambridge that a man could take honours in four Triposes in a short period of five years but it is credit to India that Inayatullah Khan of the Christ's College has accomplished the feat."

---

[2] *Allama Mashriqi & Dr. Akhtar Hameed Khan: Two Legends of Pakistan* by Nasim Yousaf, p. 72-73.

At the time of Mashriqi's graduation, the Indian Society arranged a farewell reception in honor of Mashriqi. Mashriqi addressed the gathering, stating:

"...Our educational achievements bear testimony to the fact that India can produce unparalleled brains...India is capable of producing superior brains that can make the nation's future brighter. After we return from here, we must ponder how to break the chains of slavery from the British...We should keep our vision high and enlarge our aims and goals so we can be free from the chains of slavery as soon as possible"[3] (translated into English from Urdu).

It was clear that Mashriqi had a higher vision in mind.

Job Offers and Return to India

Based on his academic achievements, Mashriqi was offered many attractive jobs in England and British India following his graduation. For instance, the Maharaja of the princely state of Alver (or Alwar) offered Mashriqi the Premiership

---

[3] *Allama Mashriqi & Dr. Akhtar Hameed Khan: Two Legends of Pakistan* by Nasim Yousaf, p. 71.

of Alver (along with an exorbitant salary, luxury car with chauffeur, staff, large bungalow, and other fringe benefits). Such benefits would have been attractive for any young person of Mashriqi's age, but Mashriqi declined them. Mashriqi was not focused on luxury or material benefits, but rather sought to change the destiny of his nation through education. It is for this reason that he decided to accept an offer from Sir George Roos-Keppel, the Chief Commissioner (equivalent to Governor) of the NWFP at the time. Sir Keppel had offered Mashriqi the position of Vice Principal of the forthcoming Islamia College in Peshawar. Mashriqi saw this role as a great opportunity to accomplish his vision of bringing a revolution to his educationally backward nation. It is important to note that Mashriqi was only twenty-four years old at the time that he was appointed to this important post.

Start at Islamia College

Allama Mashriqi returned to India in January of 1913 and formally joined Islamia College in April of 1913 as its *first* Vice Principal and Professor of Mathematics.[4] While the College was not yet

---

[4] Other subjects in which the B.A. degree was awarded: Arabic, History, Persian and Philosophy. Special buildings

ready for students, construction on some of its buildings had begun. The buildings were designed gorgeously and set on 300 acres. They were financed through a public subscription of 800,000 Rupees[5] along with "liberal assistance" from the imperial Government. Throughout the process, leading Muslims of the province provided their full support in fundraising and other aspects of the College.

Mashriqi and the other members of the staff worked hard to prepare for the opening of the College. Construction of the buildings was completed expeditiously under the supervision of Colonel W.J.D. Dundee[6] (Secretary Public Works Department) and Lt. Col. G.P. Cambell[7] (Assistant Commanding Royal Engineer, Peshawar). By October of 1913, the College was ready to open its doors, and it first began functioning with one

---

for Science and Chemistry were built. Source: *Annual Report on Public Instruction in the North-West Frontier Province for the year from 1st April 1913 to 31st March 1914*, p. 14.

[5] *Report on Public Instruction in the North-West Frontier Province for the Quinquennium from 1912-1917*, p. 02.

[6] *Report on Public Instruction in the North-West Frontier Province for the Quinquennium from 1912-1917*, p. 02.

[7] *Report on Public Instruction in the North-West Frontier Province for the Quinquennium from 1912-1917*, p. 02.

hostel and only 25 students.[8] An official report stated, *"The college opened in October 1913 with a strong staff, including three Cambridge graduates, Mr. L. Tipping, M.A., Principal, a member of the Indian Educational Service, Mr. Inayatullah Khan, Vice-Principal and Professor of Mathematics, and Mr. H.T. Bousfield, M.A., Professor of History."*[9]

Establishing the inaugural class of the College was a major endeavor that required close collaboration across a number of fronts. Indeed, Sir George Roos-Keppel[10] and Nawab Sir Sahibzada Abdul Qayyum deserve tremendous credit for selecting a

---

[8] *Report on Public Instruction in the North-West Frontier Province for the Quinquennium from 1912-1917*, p. 02.

[9] *Report on Public Instruction in the North-West Frontier Province for the Quinquennium from 1912-1917*, written by R.H. Kealy, p. 36.

[10] During the British *Raj*, many educational institutions, such as Mao College (Aligarh), Edwardes College (Peshawar), Gordon College (Rawalpindi), and FC College (Lahore), were opened.

Although their primary motivation was to introduce British culture to India and train people to run the administration, we must still give credit to the British for promoting a sense of education amongst the people of the Indian subcontinent. Regrettably, during the Mughal Empire, no emphasis was laid on education, despite the fact that the Empire had the resources to do so.

strong team to run the College. And the College administration, donors, British Government, and British officers all deserve credit for their efforts in establishing the College.

Role in Promoting Education

During its early days, the newly formed Islamia College faced a number of challenges. The college was situated in a region where acquiring an education was far from the norm, particularly for females. The conservative population in NWFP was mostly illiterate and considered it a *sin* to provide education to women. The young and enthusiastic Mashriqi knew that he would need to combat the prevailing conditions, and he served as the *main contact* between the community, local bodies, the British, and the administration in order to bring about reform.

Working with the administration for Islamia College, Mashriqi launched a rigorous campaign to change the status quo and reach out to local communities, including Afridis, Chitralis, Mahsuds, Swatis, Turis, and Wazirs. Mashriqi also guided his brother-in-law, Khan Sahib Ali

Mohammad Khan[11] - a well-respected and influential member of the Indian Educational Service (I.E.S.) and part of the NWFP department of education – to promote education. Along with community outreach, Mashriqi and the College administration also championed reforms such as incorporating religious, technical, and physical education into the curriculum and offering scholarships to students. Mashriqi was a key player in introducing these reforms.

Mashriqi and the administration's hard work brought near-immediate results. According to the *Report on Public Instruction* (NWFP, April 1, 1913 – March 31, 1914), "The hopes for very rapid progress in the expansion of education expressed by the Chief Commissioner [Sir George Roos-Keppel] last year are shown to be well founded…The increase of nearly six thousand scholars in the year 1913-14 is not only nearly double of the increase in any year since the foundation of the Province, but actually exceeds

---

[11] Khan Sahib Ali Mohammad Khan was the husband of Mashriqi's sister, Fatima Begum. He earned the title of *Khan Sahib* for his valuable services in promoting education in the NWFP. According to the *Annual Report on Public Instruction in the North-West Frontier Province from 1st April 1913 to 31st March 1914*: "His work both in administration and inspection was very good."

the total increase in the number of scholars during the whole quinquennium 1907-1912…As the year is also marked by the opening of the Islamia College and Collegiate School, both of which institutions have proved immediately successful, the outstanding feature of the year under review is undoubtedly the encouraging eagerness for education of all grades shown by the Muhammadan population of this Province."[12]

Islamia College was not only beginning to expand access to education among both males and females, but also led to the rise of other educational institutions in the region. An educational revolution was emerging in the area. Subsequent *Reports* spoke glowingly of Islamia College's contributions:

"The Islamia College and the attached Collegiate School are rendering increasingly valuable service in spreading education on the frontier" (remarks by G. Roos-Keppel, Chief Commissioner, NWFP).[13]

---

[12] *Report on Public Instruction in the North-West Frontier Province for the year from 1st April 1913 to 31st March 1914*, p. 1.
[13] *Report on Public Instruction in the North-West Frontier Province for 1914-15*, p. 2.

"The college started under the best auspices only four years ago, has attained an immediate success, which reflects great credit on the founders of the movement…"[14]

Along with the efforts of the administration, Mashriqi's organizational skills and community outreach played a pivotal role in the success of the College and the reforms it brought about.

Promotion to Principal

Mashriqi's achievements were well recognized by the College and the British rulers. Based on his performance, Mashriqi was appointed as officiating Principal in 1916, when he was only 27 years old and after only three years at the College. *The Tribune*, Lahore wrote on May 20, 1916:

"We understand that Mr. Inayatullah Khan, M.A., Vice-Principal, Islamia College, Peshawar, has been appointed to the officiating incumbency created by the departure on leave of Mr. Tipping, the Principal. Mr. Inayatullah Khan is a graduate of the Punjab University who spent several years in England and obtained high University

---

[14] *Report on Public Instruction in the North-West Frontier Province for the Quinquennium 1912-1917*, p. 2.

qualifications there. On his return home three years ago he was given the appointment of Vice-Principal in the Peshawar College where he has earned the reputation of being popular with the leaders of the Moslem community and the students of the College. His appointment to the officiating incumbency shows that his work as Vice Principal has been appreciated by the North-West Frontier Province Administration and the educational authorities including the permanent incumbent Mr. Tipping. The appointment has given satisfaction to the Mahomedans of this province, and it is hoped that in the onerous and arduous duties now entrusted to him by the Administration Mr. Inayatullah Khan will acquit himself equally well."

On April 01, 1917, Mashriqi became the permanent Principal and remained there until September 14, 1917.[15] As Principal, Mashriqi was able to further advance reforms in education in the region. Mashriqi's outstanding performance at Islamia College had caught the attention of British higher-ups, including the Viceroy and Governor-General of India, Lord Chelmsford. Within a short period of time, he was posted in place of Sir George Anderson as Under Secretary of

---

[15] *Khyber Mail* (KM) October 15-16, 1963.

Education[16] in India at the Governor General
Secretariat in Delhi. His appointment was lauded
by people from all walks of life. *The Tribune*,
Lahore reported on October 17, 1917:

"Mr. Inayatullah Khan, Vice-Principal of Islamia
College, Peshawar, who had a very distinguished
career at Cambridge, where he took a first class in
the Mathematical and the Oriental Languages
Tripos and was a scholar and prizeman at
Christ['s] College, has been appointed to officiate
as Assistant Secretary [Under Secretary] in the
Education Department of the Government of India
and will join his appointment on October 18
[1917] when Mr. G. Anderson will be placed on
special duty in connection with the Calcutta
University Commission."[17]

---

[16] Allama Mashriqi's biography was published (for the first
time) on November 23, 1934 in the first edition of *Al-Islah*
dated November 23, 1934 (*Al-Islah*, October 18, 1935, p. 2).
The biography was written by Raja Muhammad Sarfraz
Khan from Chakwal (Punjab). Sarfraz Khan was a lawyer
and Member of the Punjab Legislative Assembly. Sarfraz
Khan joined the Khaksar Tehrik on October 16, 1935 and
was appointed Salar-e-Alah on the same date (*Al-Islah*,
October 25, 1935, p. 8). Mashriqi's biography was later
published intermittently in *Al-Islah*, including *Al-Islah*,
August 30, 1935, p. 9-11, *Al-Islah*, October 18, 1935, p. 2,
and *Al-Islah*, May 19, 1939.
[17] Also see *The Tribune*, Lahore, October 31, 1917.

As Under Secretary of Education, Mashriqi not only helped Islamia College to grow, but promoted education throughout British India. On October 15, 1919, Mashriqi was inducted as a member of the prestigious Indian Educational Service (I.E.S.).[18] Mashriqi's services for the education sector earned him the respect and appreciation of the people. Thus, when he resigned from Government service to start his Khaksar Tehrik (to liberate India from British rule), the NWFP proved to be a stronghold for his party,[19] and many of his followers and admirers

---

[18] Around this time, Mashriqi was demoted to Headmaster of Government High School in Peshawar due to differences with the British Government. Mashriqi was victimized for opposing the rulers' education policy and refusing to serve British interests. Mashriqi remained closely connected with Islamia College throughout his educational career.

[19] On March 19, 1940 Allama Mashriqi was arrested and over 200 Khaksars (unofficial figure) were butchered in Lahore. On May 16, 1940, Islamia College students were absent from classes "as a mark of sympathy with the Khaksars." The students also adopted a resolution in favor of the Khaksars and conveyed this to the college authorities (*The Hindustan Times*, May 17, 1940). On May 22, 1940, the strike included shopkeepers along with students of Islamia College and other schools, who abstained from attending classes for the third consecutive day. Chants of "Allama Mashriqi Zindabad" and "Sikandar Government Murdabad" were again raised. At the Golden Mosque and the Wazir Khan Mosque, fiery speeches were made and the

still exist in the province. His work at Islamia College had helped to set the institution on a path for success. Over the years, Mashriqi stayed connected with the College, and returned there to deliver a speech on November 20, 1928. An excerpt of this speech is provided below:

"When I first decided to join it (Islamia College, Peshawar) I had a clear idea in my mind that the institution could be productive of good results to the Muslims as a whole. I could even then picture in my imagination a community of sane, smart and thinking men molded out of the illiterate Afghan crowding towards its corridors with the eagerness shown by him in attending the cake and fruit parties and pocketing the knowledge gained at its doors with the same frankness which sometimes he shows in appropriating other people's share on such occasions. I could then picture at a not very distant date a University extending far towards the alive gates of Khyber from the dead stupa of the Kushans, bringing eager Afghans from Samarkand and Kabul, a library with Pushto and Persian manuscripts of Khushal Khan, Farabi and Newton

---

removal of the ban and the immediate release of Mashriqi was demanded. During the speeches, the Khaksars said that the only person who could order a halt to the demonstrations was Allama Mashriqi himself (*The Tribune,* May 23, 1940; *The Hindustan Times*, May 23, 1940).

side by side with the English translations of Laplace and Einstein, and Oriental Faculty transmuting the base Mullah into the gold of Progress and onward march handling a Quran mathematically proved as the guide torch of all learning and the climax of the guides to Human Wisdom's light house, a people producing orators vying with Cicero, Syed Ahmed and Burke in their deliverances, a community of newly grown people bursting forth exuberance and richness of natural thought uncared and unwatered and unattended as in newly and deeply furrowed land. I cannot say that the dream is altogether realised after 15 years but that it is even now as real as it was is not far from truth, and much of what I believed and worked for in the beginning is done and what remains undone is bound to come steadily with the march of time."[20]

Indeed, Allama Mashriqi and the other founders' pioneering work at Islamia College left behind a strong foundation. Mashriqi himself was associated with education in India (in different

---

[20] "Mashriqi's choice," 1988, *Scan* (Weekly), p. 14. Also see *Allama Mashriqi & Dr. Akhtar Hameed Khan: Two Legends of Pakistan* by Nasim Yousaf, p.79-80.

capacities[21]) for nearly 17 years and stayed connected with the College during this time. Islamia College continued to blossom throughout the years and became a symbol of academic excellence. In 1950, the University of Peshawar was founded as an extension of the College. The College has had a tremendous impact on the region, producing countless graduates in both public and private service as well as some of the leading politicians in the country. Its magnificent buildings are wonderful monuments in Pakistan (the main building is printed on Pakistani currency notes of different denominations and postage stamps) and a constant reminder of the College's pursuit of excellence in education.

On the 100th anniversary of Islamia College, Allama Mashriqi, Sir George Roos-Keppel, L. Tipping, Nawab Sir Sahibzada Abdul Qayyum, and others who contributed to the establishment of this great institution deserve tremendous credit for the transformation they brought about in education in the region.

---

[21] During Government service in Peshawar, Mashriqi also served as Principal of a Training College and Director of Education.

Photos

Allama Mashriqi in His Youth

Islamia College, Peshawar

Islamia College, Peshawar

About the Author

Nasim Yousaf is a distinguished intellectual, scholar, and historian, who has been conducting extensive research on the freedom movement in British India since 1996. He is known for his bold statements and open and courageous style of writing. Mr. Yousaf comes from a famous and highly respected family of the Indian sub-continent. He is a grandson of Allama Mashriqi, whose book (*Tazkirah*, a commentary on the Holy Quran) was nominated for the Nobel Prize in Literature, and a nephew of Nobel Peace Prize Nominee Dr. Akhtar Hameed Khan.

Mr. Yousaf has written extensively on Allama Mashriqi and Dr. A.H. Khan as well as other topics related to the Indian subcontinent's history. He has presented papers at U.S. conferences and published many books and numerous articles (which have appeared in newspapers in countries round the world, including Bangladesh, Canada, India, Japan, Norway, Pakistan, Sweden, United Kingdom, and the USA). He has also contributed pieces to renowned journals and encyclopedias, including *Harvard Asia Quarterly*, *Pakistaniaat* and the *World History Encyclopedia* (ABC-CLIO, USA, 2011). His most recent work is entitled *Dr. Akhtar Hameed Khan - Pioneer of Microcredit &*

Guru of Rural Development. Mr. Yousaf's forthcoming book, *Mahatma Gandhi & My Grandfather, Allama Mashriqi*, is a groundbreaking account of the role of two frontline leaders in the struggle for India's freedom.

Additional publications the author is currently working on (tentative titles):
(1) *Allama Mashriqi Narrowly Escapes the Gallows*
(2) *World Famous Personalities in Microfinance and Poverty Alleviation: Nobel Prize Nominee Dr. Akhtar Hameed Khan, Nobel Prize Laureate Professor Muhammad Yunus and President Barack Obama's Mother, Dr. S. Ann Dunham*
(3) *Allama Mashriqi's Historic Address at Islamic Conference in Cairo (1926)*
(4) *Dr. Akhter Hameed Khan — A Hero and Victim of Pakistani Blasphemy Law*
(5) *Air Commodore M. Zafar Masud – A Pioneer of the Pakistan Air Force*

Author's Family

Scholar and historian Nasim Yousaf's family consists of his wife, son, two daughters, and son-in-law. His wife, Ambereen, works in a management position at a large Fortune 500 corporation in the U.S.A. The author's son, Zain, obtained his MBA from New York University's Stern School of Business, an MS in Management from Rensselaer Polytechnic Institute, and a Bachelor's degree in Economics from Cornell University. His youngest daughter, Myra, recently obtained her Bachelor's degree from Pennsylvania State University and works for a prestigious company in the US. The author's eldest daughter, Mehreen, holds a dual-degree MBA from Columbia University Business School and London Business School, an MS in Global Affairs from New York University, and a BS in Industrial and Labor Relations from Cornell University. His son-in-law, Hussain, married to his eldest daughter, attained his MBA from the University of Chicago's Booth School of Business and has a Bachelor of Science (BS) degree in Chemical Engineering from the University of Illinois at Urbana-Champaign.

For more information and updates on the author's works, visit the resources listed below.

Websites

http://www.allamamashraqi.com/grandsonarticles.html
http://www.nasimyousaf.info

Facebook:
http://www.facebook.com/nasimyousaf.26

Index

www.ingramcontent.com/pod-product-compliance
Lightning Source LLC
Chambersburg PA
CBHW030030290326
41934CB00005B/569